Previous winners of the Vassar Miller Prize in Poetry
Scott Cairns, Contest Director

A · M · E · R · I · C · A · N

crawl

POEMS BY **Paul Allen**

University of North Texas Press
Denton, Texas

Permissions:
University of North Texas Press
PO Box 13856
Denton TX 76203

The paper used in this book meets the minimum requirements of the
American National Standard for Permanence of Paper for Printed Library
Materials, z39.48.1984. Binding materials have been chosen for durability.

Library of Congress Cataloging-in-Publication Data

Allen, Paul, 1945–
    American crawl / Paul Allen.
        p.   cm.
    ISBN 1-57441-027-X
    I. Title.
PS3551.L39677A83   1997
811' .54—dc21   96-49504
                                                                        CIP

Design by Amy Layton
Cover art, "Keeper of the Door,"
by Jere Allen

acknowledgments

Grateful acknowledgment is made to the editors of the following publications where some of these poems first appeared: *Ascent*: "American Crawl" and "Letting the Rabbit Scream"; *The Chariton Review*: "Attack"; *College English*: "This Year"; *Crazyhorse*: "My Daughter's House" and "Pickup"; *Iowa Review*: "Dear Friend," and "Rope" (under the title "Sabbatical"); *Laurel Review*: "His Breakfast" (under the title "Miss Rose Chisolm, Lois Day. Miss Rose Chisolm and Lois Day!"); *A Local Muse 2*: "Grabbing"; *Madison Review*: "A Self-Admit"; *New American Writing*: "Come Home"; *New England Review and Bread Loaf Quarterly*: "One up by Clayton"; *The North American Review*: "Tattoo #47, 'Happy Dragon'"; *Northwest Review*: "Hypothesis Contrary to Fact" and "Note for in the Morning"; *Ontario Review*: "The Man with the Hardest Belly"; *Poet Lore*: "Youngblood Tells Beekman and Jimmy Jr. about Crow"; *Poet & Critic*: "Judy"; *Poetry Northwest*: "Natural Causes"; *Southern Poetry Review*: "At the Lake House"; *Texas Review*: "Finishing the Well"; *Zone 3*: "The Day Spike Eisland Went Home."

"Youngblood Tells Beekman and Jimmy Jr. about Crow" is the recipient of the John Williams Andrews Narrative Poetry Prize.

Some of these poems also appear in anthologies: "The Man with the Hardest Belly," *Odd Angles of Heaven* (Harold Shaw Publishers); "One up by Clayton," "The Day Spike Eisland Went Home," "Tattoo #47, 'Happy Dragon,'" *45/96: The Ninety-Six Sampler of South Carolina Poetry* (Ninety-Six Press, Furman University); "Hypothesis Contrary to Fact," the Thirtieth Anniversary Issue of *Northwest Review*; "Youngblood Tells Beekman and Jimmy Jr. about Crow," *Open Door: A Poet Lore Anthology (1980–1996)*.

The title "Even the Sparrow Has Found a Home" is from Psalm 84.

The epigraph for this book, "Greatness and Glory" by William Bronk, is from *Living Instead*, North Point Press, 1991. Used with author's permission.

I would like to thank the Mary Roberts Rinehart Fund (George Mason University) for a grant to complete this book, the College of Charleston for sabbatical leave, and the South Carolina Arts Commission for a grant and an Individual Artist Fellowship to work on some of these poems. Particular thanks to the family of James Kaiser Youngblood, who opened their land to me.

Greatness and Glory

Called great is the gift that makes prize boys
and beauty queens, gift thought to be
a Grace of God given to a special few
—oddly chosen though it sometimes seems—
but chosen, and the favor something theirs that they have.

And then we find that kind of favor pursued
ardently and avidly or a favor like
that favor with a little luck is also ours
in our own right if we work hard enough.

And we can wear it around and show those
others, we can bully the world or modestly
blush beneath the medals and honors we earned
for ourselves, accepting the glory with becoming grace,
mistaking ours for the glory of the world.
                                        And there is
a glory of the world.
                    And it isn't ours to have.

William Bronk
Living Instead

For Constance Douglass Allen

contents

PROEM: rope

I

I'm not expecting anything again.
Still I check the mail, early afternoon
heading toward the street looking for sign—
fresh tracks in the sand under the box,
scalloped tire marks tying neighbor to neighbor,
all flags down up to the cul-de-sac.
She has been here—the delivery woman,
the Post Mistress, Post Person—whatever name
she is known by now, she has come. And whatever
is in there now is all there will be today.

I've seen him before. A man from one of the even
numbers across the street is coming, breathing hard,
tied to his daughter with rope around his middle.
She holds on, roars on her skateboard. She does not
swing wide enough to miss the sandy delta of my drive
that empties into the street. I should sweep all that back—
unsightly, and now, I see, dangerous for daughters
pulled by their fathers for a rad ride. She falls
into me, gets up. We're all a little embarrassed.

I'm sorry. I'm sorry. I'm very sorry.
She picks up her board, heads home shaken and unhurt.
She has no whim to help him with his limp tether.
His nod to me is that of two guys, two strangers,
who have relieved themselves side by side at a rest stop
on the interstate and meet at the sink to wash.

I wonder whether all fathers look the fool
when daughters leave them standing like a fool.
This one does. He starts toward his house, fumbling
with the knot at his side. The rope uncoils
behind him, begins to follow him home.

II

It is not this incident alone, but from the little town
on the border of my home state, Crazy Jimmy pulls
me to him again, as he has done a half dozen times
this year. (Too much time, I guess, to brood
and drink and watch the local artists on *Midday.*)
Something bad had happened to him in The Great War,
thinking the smell of new-mown hay
was the smell of new-mown hay
and not the gas that would make him gather cardboard boxes,
pile them high on his bicycle. The streets were his.
Even for the best drivers, my old man said, Jimmy
might impose on their right of way. He died at the V.A.
My father joined other men to clear out Jimmy's place,
men who had crossed the river before on other matters—
to hunt, and, as Mother said, to gamble their life's savings.

This time all the men came back with rope.
Dad served supper: Jimmy had things hanging in the trees.
Plow, ax, harrow, hand and band saw, a fuse box, tubs
(two tubs). But nothing that could be repaired or used,
except the rope. Pie pans were nailed to the pine, up
the trunk then out the first and largest limb. Two
toilets, a skillet, and 16 wing nuts bunched in an oak
like wind chimes. What with the bicycle and boxes,
we knew the man was strange, but not like that.
Strange as if at home he might eat dog.
Strange as if his place were all too neat.

Something else Dad told us one by one at different times,
mostly when one of us would help him in the yard
or when we found him, late nights, downstairs in the kitchen
taking a bourbon to help him get some sleep:
Jimmy had not lived alone out there.
Whoever it was had gone. But there were undisputed
signs of someone else. Whoever it was that helped
him hoist that junk, whoever lay with him evenings
listening to the housewares in the trees
had disappeared. Or had slipped into our midst.
When we crossed the street, left the doctor's office, stepped
into the blinding light after the double-feature matinee—
someone we were looking at was she. Who she was
was anybody's guess. And we did, naming first
the homely and alone, and then, in time we all
suspected everyone in some way or another.
He hadn't lived alone; she walked among us—
about this we felt better, and worse.

III

Why that odd and arbitrary thing comes now
I do not know. Or why it has come a lot
this year. Or ever, even the first time.
It doesn't matter, and I feel foolish for standing
this long holding my mailbox by its warped jaw.
My neighbor follows his daughter to their home.
It is odd how he stops in the road, stops
at the edge of his Yard-of-the-Month, stops
on the last step of his home—how he seems
to insist on getting the knot untied before
stepping into the dark doorway where his daughter
has gone on to other games. I go in, not waiting
to see whether he gets himself loose.
For me it's late enough for a beer
and a quiet romp through the mail.
Resident. Occupant. And an I-may-already-have-won.

american crawl

one up by clayton

Upstate they handled drought their own ways
this year. They broke off corn stalks, picked
clods and winnowed them through their fingers
on all three major networks, and *Nightline*.

One up by Clayton used a .22 to make
a hole over his left eye. The half-
hour it took him to die, he slammed
against the etagère, knocked the clock

with the passage of scripture off the wall.
He fell to the rug, got up. He held on
to the latch and bent over at the back door
for at least a minute, like he was thinking,

like he was studying the dull boards
in the floor, how they were starting
to separate. He went outside and wiped
a cobweb off the post that was coming loose

on the porch. He sat on the last step.
He walked to the gate, dropped his wallet
through the grating on the cow-catcher.
He crossed the road and leaned on the Bixby

mailbox, hard, then died in the run-off.
There wasn't any mystery to it. On the local
stations, his friends knew exactly what happened
by what he broke, or smeared. Where he'd started to bruise.

dear friend,

Your letter about the land ruined,
    your Guggenheim ended,
and how it seems there's busy-ness
    plaguing you, like gnats when

you were 12 with a bad backlash
    in your bass reel, sweating,
a keeper gone free in the slack:
    I don't know what to say.

Me, more and more I imagine
    Leon. He's black. His thumbs
are gone. So are his shoe laces.
    I dream we live up-state.

His place outlives us half a mile
    down the neglected road
fringed with condoms and Cheetos bags
    from the teens. We drink when

one of us has something with bite
     enough to see us through
the P.M. on my gritty porch
     to dark. His wife's fishing, mine's with

some friends. We don't say much. Our legs
     hang off the edge. If we
do talk, it's to speculate on
     the wasp nest overhead

and the several ways to down it
     if I take a notion.
(This dream, though, it's copacetic.)
     By dark we're dumb mumblers

who've jerry-rigged our day, our lives,
     standing to our full height
only to piss at the county
     road. He shows me some things—

his Social Security card,
     photo of hauling dung
for the Army mules near Boulogne,
     the title to his truck.

I tell him how I owe people,
     and my poems aren't coming.
"Fug 'em," he spits. "Fuck them." That's that?
     Back to wasps and a whiz.

But you—*sans* a Leon—who knows?
　　You might try suicide,
delighting in ways. Hell, my friend,
　　I've thought of six or eight,

counting acetone and putty.
　　I thought I'd write to pick
you up. Don't guess this helps.
　　One day I'll send Leon's address,

if I ever find it. I know
　　it's here some place. Or there.
Meanwhile, do whatever. Go out,
　　stay in. Get a tattoo.

hypothesis contrary to fact

(John Ciardi, 1916–1986)

If someone could have passed his dying on
to a boy, then him to the boy at the shop
with the locked thumb (boating accident)
or skied down slope to use my phone

to tell someone who ought to be told,
I could have overheard. But to open it
like a better Montrachet when I am spending
a quiet evening alone, letting the news

breathe as I warmed the bread, turned back
later to find it flat. Tabled. An assumption.
I loved him too in his own way. I.e.
there were some poems, small but bright

enough to show up in the oil pan on Sunday
afternoons; or they filled holes when
I countersunk screws on my shelves late.
Some of them stayed with me awhile, but not

in reverie, nor making love. Not then.
If there were another life (as if there ever
is) he banged a boot in it of a morning—
in Arizona, say—by the river, freeing

a scorpion. That day he would not wonder
what he would be doing had he stayed east,
played a long run in *The Man Who Was*, or
Peck's Bad Boy with the Chicago Play Company.

After the performance, he would have kissed
his whore full on the mouth to horrify
all who'd come to see her die of consumption
in her dressing room. Or maybe not.

And maybe that is what is: Not to think
about the life you aren't living for
the dullard down south you don't know, and how
he didn't hear of how you didn't growl one day.

When I awoke last Saturday, a child
I've grown not to know sat with a box
of Trix on the floor of our bedroom.
The sound was down enough on channel 4

to wake me slowly, like an interrogation
going on two cells away. The tint and contrast
had been defiled, and I awoke to a red man,
still living, holding to a blue cliff.

finishing the well

Thirty-three feet down
we finished the well
by hand. Five of us
took turns with the post
hole digger: "Got to
spread them handles,"
Beekman had shouted
from what small light sky
gave, "Spread them lady's legs."

Now, a case of Blue
Ribbon into our
last night of the well,
dared, Beekman pours gas
from a feed bucket
down the center, primes
the hole for the hell
of it, makes a can-
non of the land. But
Blue Diamond kitchen
matches die before
the topsoil ends, die

before clay or boot
prints filling up. Beekman,
the oldest, brings
a torch, half a barn
broom soaked in gas. We
see our faces now,
his hand and his jeans.
He throws it in (or
down) like a bass too
small to keep, and dead
besides. The blast rocks
us stunned to our rumps,
burns the canopy
that has kept the sun
at bay all July,
shakes up Hercules
(this year's steer, last shot
at "Best of Show"). But
up here, hunched around
the rim on knees and
forearms, we wonder
what we have done, what
has been done down there.

We drink while she cools.

Then Beekman wraps rope
around his middle,
goes first. We lose him

in smoke after five
or six feet: Our hands
burn till we feel slack.
From below he calls,
his voice hoarse and old:
"Smells like Birmingham. . . .
Can't see a damned thing. . . .
Gets you dizzy. . . . Pull
me up, I'm near sick. . . ."

We haul him back. He
is quiet, his loose
arms (armpits haired) tell
us he's drunker, changed.
He is limp and changed.

We want to be next.

The pulley giggles,
then, as one by one
we rise from the earth,
or let ourselves down
to take turns breathing.

grabbing

Again you've made it past the bull,
you and Philip, and take a leak in the woods
between pasture and river.
You piss on the salt lick,

strip. Always neater,
Philip hangs his pants on the fence
that cuts through the oak and lays
his shirt on his pants, arms out.
When he peels his shorts,
he opens the legs wider to keep leaves
from falling off his feet into the crotch.
His shorts go in the back pocket.

Twenty yards downstream, catfish—
some big as a grown man's thigh—
sleep under the soapstone ledge
where the river bends, waiting
for the two of you to let yourselves down
root by root into the slow water,
the cold bottom in some places
as far off as winter.

And this is grabbing, the kind of fishing
your mothers forbid, over their dead
bodies. You move downstream,
one arm reaching under the ledge,
the other holding you out.

Sometimes, like now, you luck on a shark's tooth
stuck in the soapstone. You forget
grabbing, forget catfish and Philip,
and let your legs drift under
the ledge like another's body, like
a corpse, while you use both hands
above water to pick it out. No pockets,
you rinse the tooth and hoard it
in your mouth.
Philip is on to something.
His face against the bank,
his "Good God a'mighty" whispers
out of the limestone itself.
You let the current catch you up.
You start at his shoulder, your hand
moving to his, and you too feel
the slick belly of the fish.
Under there the gills open slowly;
Philip jerks. His shoulder and arm
surface, shiver like a sea monster
dying. And then he brings the thing up—
eight maybe ten pounds. Blood-slime hangs
from Philip's grip, and thick slots of gill.

You swim to the sandbar where the stone
bank ends and praise your fish
and tooth. Gnats drive you off.
You wash, take the land route back
to your clothes in the dusk.
High over the bank you've fished,
the shadows of leaves and the leaves
are one. Vines cut your arm pits,
and you protect your privates—you say
so Raw-Head-and-Bloody-Bones won't bite it off.
The sun has gone downstream.
Philip's hand is the fish.
You don't open your fist
to check the tooth. (You'd never find
it in this dark and brush.)
You just trust it to be there
when you get to your clothes.

american crawl

Drowning in an oral surgeon's slough, Lake Martin.
To swim from the dock to the shallow bar, out to the flag
that warns lawyers their sons on slalom could break
a leg, and they would be obliged to toss thin Gimlets
overboard and rev twin Mercuries to the bone man's lot.

In this lake of families I forgot myself—the smokes,
the beer, the hours under the light, the hours
in strange towns looking for lights—and thought
I could make it. Didn't think.

Swim. My sister is doing o.k., saving her hair.
Her husband, who reconstructs mandibular joints,
is doing o.k. The boy from Stuttgart they swapped
their son for this summer is half there.
They are making it.

But I am not there, not even close. I see trees
over my elbow. The red bank tells me the dam
has given power to Eclectic and Wetumpka. The people
are saving their cukes and don't mind paying for it,
by God. So the man who controls the gates

has his orders. Somewhere around Kawliga down
the channel, the old river the Creeks lived on,
he is calling home and waiting for a light
to come on. He is resting his feet in a middle drawer.

I try it, to walk. A bad election. My foot
paws cold space like a white gelding counting his years
for a party in the mayor's yard. I am still in
too deep and sidle to the surface. Barely. Choke.
My privates are shrinking, and it's not funny.
I can't level off anymore. Like a slow low-rider
in Texas I know what I look like pulling
half of me, half of me dragging me down
to silt. The slender arms I wished for dry
have turned on me, like all prayers, into a horror
of slapping saplings falling on no meaningful water.

I learn now that giving up is not a matter of giving up.
There is paddling slowly for all I am worth,
tossing whichever arm wills toward air, dropping it,
kicking one leg, letting the other leg drag to a state,
to a kind of dream of paddling, of trees over my arm.
Even the real at the end of the dream is a dream—
my foot touching the feathers of tree limbs, snags,
then the thudding hump of land in a warm spot.

Such a let down coming out is, crawling to the three
who are laughing, leaning back in six inches on their elbows.
Like a lesson in perspective in Continuing Education art class,
I am looking down the roads of their spread legs.

The visitor from Germany offers a florescent
audacity at the vanishing point. I was kidding, wasn't I?
I was never in any real trouble, was I?
That was rich, the way I did and all. Rich.

I am (they tell me sunning), I am (in this world
of professionals), they can swear—my sister, my brother-in-law,
their exchanged student—oh Lord, like they have always said,
I am a hoot. I am a regular Goddamn riot.

at the lake house

If the sun were out, your tanned foot
propped on the porch rail
would look less like rust.
Our children's swimsuits
with hourglass crotches
twisted on the line
would be dry,
and we would have drunk
our beers, now flat. But rain
already in "the view"
and coming
has changed everything.

Our piney lot
smells like the brochure,
and our boat, chosen
because speed had mattered so,
hangs hoisted over the water.
Under the crush of sky,
birds stay down.

Behind us in the light,
saved by the glass doors,
our children clack cards,
the Rook deck, and teach
their friends the rules,
reading, "The object of each
player is to run out of cards. . . ."

while we are left out here
where birds are grounded,
barometers watching
how the world is now.

The rain will come, will blow
under these eaves.
Until then we sit,
our toes gripping the middle rail.

my daughter's house

Rather than thud to sleep on the couch again
watching the Jap slap Sarge on channel 3
for the truth, or Brother Amos sign us
off, all cancers cured,
I invade my daughter's chair
and occupy her doll house—
a golem in a knit shirt.

Upstairs the baby is propped
on kicking legs against the trash can
(a thimble), and the mother irons a shirt
in the kitchen. The father waves
good-by from the yard.

They have been living like this for a week.

With my daughter and wife asleep,
I station my bourbon in the garage
and deploy my hands to the study,
to the living room, as I have seen her do.
It's no good. Nothing's to scale, nothing
I touch in there belongs where it fits.

Somewhere in the dark my own home pops,
and the squirrels in the wall wake to chew wires.
I raise my glass to what I have done,
to what I've left for her to set right:

Baby's awake in her crib, and Dad
sleeps with his tie too tight, painted to the neck.
Beside him, Mom, one arm up,
keeps reaching for the next shirt.

youngblood tells beekman and jimmy jr. about crow

I'll tell you what I know, but it's no use,
you'll have to learn another way to make
it true for you. Today you're going to kill
crow. (Watch yourself; I have to get there.)
I'll stay home and try to make the creek
go east a hundred yards or so and back
up just beyond those pin oaks there.
Besides, I got no use for shooting crows,
but that's no reason you two boys should stay.

The sun will do me good. Miss Evelyn likes
me home. Now when you get there (move) stand
for a little while away from your guns, say
over by old Doc Allison's truck. You watch,
the men will end up there, so that puts you
in with them so to speak, but not too eager.
When they break up to get themselves a stand,
you two go together. It's not like killing
dove where you want to get a stand that lets
you have a larger field of vision—alone
and still, you can have a dove. She'll come for you,

but crow—you ought to be in shadow or down
for crow, or under something like a pine—
something man put there so the crow's accustomed.
And you will call them in to you.

See what you got to do is wound one soon
as possible, a young one full of fear
and hurt, that still has strength with number 6
in his gut, one who'll fall but doesn't know
enough to die and flops and carries on.
His flapping and loud dying helps you out.
The old ones (Watch yourself), it seems the fall
kind of hurts them special; they bleed in the throat
and don't say anything and give up quick.
I've known it to happen. They just don't seem to care.
But aim true, now. I'm not saying miss.
You will, though. One you'll only hurt, and that's
your one. (Take this.) Tie him to a piece
of board out a ways; too close to you
and he'll be too still, too far and he'll feel alone
and won't do much. Nineteen, twenty feet
and he'll know you're there and try to get away.

That one will bring a hundred in to you,
and you'll get your fill of shooting, all you want.
Crows can't stand the suffering of their own—
like folks at a wreck. They're not coming to help;
they're not like doves. You shoot a dove, you get
her right then, run back. Hide her, like.
But let a shot crow, dead or hurt, just lay.

(I've got what I need here. Hop in. I'll take
you far as the gate. Blow that cup out and pour
me one from this. I've got work to do.)
Crows are close to us if evolution
is not made up. That's why you need to hunt
them in the spirit of fun. What about
"He had to eat crow," when they mean embarrassed
and having to take back something he spoke out?
A bunch of crows is a "murder." Did you know that?
Now there's a human word if ever was.
Of course don't call them that around the men;
they'll think you're like that woman here last spring
on her "study." Or how about that famous crow
in ancient days that sat on a picture of Jesus
and kept on saying "Never mind?" (Your window.)
I don't know if crows can really talk,
but they know what to say if they're a mind.
Don't matter.
        Some fancy britches may come out
from town that brings a silly record player
calling crow. Crap. More than most
animals, crows just can't decide how to live.
Coon, 'possum—they've gone ahead and claimed
garbage cans and attics in old homes.
They look so dead on Old Towne Road.
But crows do want us so, just can't adjust.
So they like those records of men acting like crows.
If the others let him have the record player,
you just come on back. Might as well walk down
to the pond and shoot cow pies all day; or help
me, I could use a hand. (Hold this.)

It won't matter whether you kill or not.
You'll probably be the youngest, so the main
thing is to keep your barrel hot; the men,
they'll gather back at Doc Allison's truck,
form a natural circle and they'll spit,
sort of put the whole day in the center
and look at it awhile. If you killed enough,
they'll say it. They always put the youngest boys
like you, who's hardly started hair there yet,
inside the day and rib him. That's good. Be glad.
They'll let you know you did o.k. by them.
Like one will say, "Young Beekman's got the eye."
And they'll say, "Yep." And "Yep." And "Jimmy Junior's
rare on a 20." Even if you don't
kill, and you will, so long's you did all right
they'll say something. They'll say you started a legend
for the county, setting the whole damn sky on fire.
Just keep your barrel hot. But only on crow.

But what the men can't stand is indecision—
waffling at the kill, farting around.
Like ducking when a braver crow dives down
to see the wounded crow from how you see it.
Or worse, being squat down and pointing
at one coming out of the sun and failing to shoot
because another's heading toward the sun,
you swing around to him but a big one's coming
straight at you and one behind, and then
you've lost your balance and plump down on your ass
and all those crows go back to where they came

and you've had grandaddy's gun in all directions
and nothing's dead except the sky and your story.
They'll be quiet on you then at the truck.

(O.K. Here. I'd best not turn her off.
She might sit and I would lose a day.
You got time; I'll just finish this off.)
You'll do all right. I can't tell you nothing.
I've said more than I thought to anyway.
I've got work to do, and you got crow.
I've told you more than I ever said to that gal
from Vanderbilt, and she had a government grant
to ask about place names in Alabama.
And she was from Ohio, anyway.
Selma. Or-ville. Minter. Car-low-ville.
You should have heard the way she read that list.
She ought to make a record, might bring in crow.
I gave her names. Made them up right there,
but she didn't know it; shows you what she knew:
Poot Holler. Stump Broke. Slap-Your-Pappy.
Miss Evelyn didn't speak to me for two days,
but I gave her the money anyway for the house.
Place names! And her with no true place to be.
That kind of thing ought to be done by some woman
whose children are moved off and she's lived there.
I ought not story so, I guess. Get gone.
Pull the handle hard. You boys do good,
then come on home and tell me how you did.

attack

"I don't know what the hell's the matter with me. Here we are right at the front, and yet the war isn't dramatic to me at all."

—Ernie Pyle, *Here Is Your War*

Expecting their orders any time,
some of the men
glassed in over the Atlantic
spot trouble at 1:00 o'clock:

a man, a woman, a daughter.
The man is drunk.
They take their tight formation
up the coastline
past the mossy bellies,
the red, white, and blue *v*s.
He is out of trim.

The men watching him
correct their children
slinging crab dip from Captains Wafers.

The wing man below them
veers off, up toward the cloud bank

of dunes—
to the dry sand and sea oats
before the dunes.

In weakening signals
of thick plates and silver plate,
seasoned by their own missions,
they know what Lone Ranger hopes for.
They know no matter what kids pack
in trunks to stink even before Kentucky,
they are the chipped and faded pieces,
served from sea to the people
and back, discarded.
And back. And back.
The sea gives
relentlessly.

So the man is looking for something better—
skate's egg with all four prongs,
the unidentifiable, the perfect conch,
some find that tells his daughter
the old man can fix the house,
they do not owe anything,
the wiring works,
she loves him even with rat
on his hands. The men know
there are such finds up there,
away from the high tide line,
away from the low tide line.
Storms leave them.

He finds
the flotsam of himself
in nesting terns—groups, squadrons,
bandits of outraged terns.
Like P-38s over Bizerte
in his father's war,
they use the sun, put him
in their cross-hairs,
make their run,
pull out.

Fixing a course between water and state
line after state line home
he lumbers on. Wave after wave
of terns scramble, attack. He waves
to his daughter, his daughter and wife:
Come see this. See how they dive
at me. You cannot take this home,
but look how they care. They are saving
their babies from me.

The Atlantic lets the daughter go.
She joins the terns.
Her flapping arms
say *Why? Why?*
Leave them alone.
Leave them alone.
Leave everything alone.

The mother comes up from the sea.
Her free hand

says, *Who do you think you are?*
You're scaring her.
We didn't come here for this.
She shifts the towels and Mae West.
The women go back to their original plan,
walking the edge of the water.
Leveling off now, the father
watches them long enough
for the terns to land
then returns to the sea
where his daughter shows him a shell
from out of the foam. A debriefing.

The men have come a long way
from home for this house special
with home fries. Their orders arrive.
Like men in restaurants everywhere,
they look at their food
as if they can't remember
what they ordered.

Then they begin,
picking at their Captain's Platter,
salvaging what they can
of what their families were saying.

this year

Because his sons are in the living room
forgiving him, they are in all rooms,
terrified, where he could not find them
out of his head last Christmas,
thank God. He has not asked where they hid—
huddled, breathless—from him.

So room to room through the seasons
whatever door he has entered
they have been behind it: here,
the whole house, K-Mart, Minnesota—
always in the farthest corner,
the back of the cattle car.
Their fingers untangle the lights
tonight, replacing bulbs burned out
while off throughout the year.
Yet even now in other rooms, he knows,
they are hiding, their wide eyes
the eyes of the porcelain soldiers
that broke on their own in the months.

By way of apology, he tries
to make no sudden moves this year,

nor does he let them catch him
staring long at anything breakable.
He does not know what else to do,
or what gets into him.

natural causes

Degrees of the unspeakable act: rough times,
bad marriages, found photographs of the little girl next door,
the little boy next door—these are obvious, understandable,
and a shame. These lock themselves in bathrooms
and blast their brains into vent fans or their veins
in tubs.

       Others, because they are experts
at surviving their specialties, are more suspect.
Only this once they offer the probable mistakes we will allow.
They slip on edges. They grab hot lead wires.
They lose their footing in the gravel on the shoulders of the I
and dance into the lights of pickups and Hondas,
or themselves in pickups and Hondas, put teeth
into the arguments for bond issues to widen county bridges.
Having hunted all their lives, these are the ones
who marvel briefly at bright ice on the worst way
to jerry-rig the gate latch, then go in for bourbon
and a long bath. Cleaned up, though, they think better
of it, refine it. They slip the modified chokes
from their palates, destroy the maudlin notes, and set
their tables with gun oil, socks soaked in tung oil,

toothbrushes for the mechanisms. Then they
blow their guts out on the off-chance their bad accidents
will teach their sons some late brief lesson that will matter:
It's always the unloaded gun that kills, and such.
If the agents are young enough and on their toes,
these can be found out, and are, in larger cities.
Older agents in smaller towns just drop the checks off
on their way to Lions Club.

                    But surely we
have all known others who did not slam the doors
of their untenable, sad houses. They had lain awake
since four feeling the itch in the ear, neck, armpit,
side, and knew it was coming. Finally that morning
was the last morning. They prayed for strength to make it
look good by looking ordinary, by seeming fit.
They made themselves get up to sauté onions and peppers
for Sunday's omelets before the IV of hot bacon grease
and bread crumbs could bash them to the red tiles,
where we, panicked, would breathe air into their bellies.
These paid off. That they did not sound
the truck horns, that phones were beside them on the hook,
that they did not call out or crash lamps—these
gave us a surety they didn't suffer. It's how we'd want
to go. (Just so, if that makes us feel better.)

But maybe the days that brought it on
were the reasons to want it done with. Maybe
they felt the crunch in the chest as the knife
dropped from the dirty lunch plates they handed us.
It made them think they ought to check the cows.

They walked through the reprehensible health of winter
hoping to put the first rise between them
and our windows before their knees buckled in brittle grass.
As women who tire of waiting past due date wash cars
to bring an end, they did something—mowed,
rotated tires, joined the fun-run—gambling
we would not see the neck purple
before they could get a good start. If so, they knew
and left no notes, nothing the young agents could trace,
no shame in the house. In '57, '63, last year,
maybe our fathers and uncles, aunts, mothers, our brother
who would try anything, our brother's wife
who turned up her nose at everything—maybe they
were heroes without parapets or storms to go mad in.
They simply sat quietly, gritting their teeth
through the last white noise after the last late movie.
Nothing to find later except the nothing they left
and whatever they might have said,
why it was only last week they were saying . . . .

a self-admit

1. *Rec Room*

"But ah, the strawberries . . . ." (*Caine Mutiny*)

Those of us
who function at all
anymore,
for the nonce,
sit before
the inevitable window—
foothills and the lovely
yes-ah-tsk-there-that.

Plexiglas, scratched,
the window bothers Glenn.
In the right light,
to him it rains
that side of the building.

Everybody agrees

this view makes you
come back to the session—

our wife's blunders,
our husband's under
the car and it would
have been a minor thing
to say he is sorry
is that too much to ask
I ask you?

The animal privates
of hills, those round blue
ballocks of the Smokies,
delights of space,
bring us to sanity.

The trouble today
is the cup,
the coffee nobody
put there. We'll need
another week
at least
to deal with
the cup.

2. *Lamp*

Aboriginal delight.
To have scratched

a deal
for the likes

of this sand painting
motif, 60 watt
burial urn.
Someone
changed earth

to ugly lamp
that claims $\frac{1}{4}$ the mesa
of my desk space.

Several people,
several
well meaning people
per day

grow crook-backed
and bad ankled
rag picking
the dump
of my mouth.

Their great delight's
the small bits,
the bright
reds and greens
in the margins
of their own
jottings as we own
up. No make-up

among these plain people,
Christianized
heathens
living at the gates.
They want us to believe
their pidgin
hearing.

But what
flat-head in the badlands
was enough brave
to send the lamp
I write this by?
And is he
laughing all the way
to the weigh in,

having turned
(I'm guessing)
to wrestling,
finding himself—
after a half-life
of bad lighting—
the shape
of his authentic
lamp with a cord
too short for us
to hang ourselves.

3. *Visitors*

Not
what you'd think
with families
and laughing.

The equipment
of our minds
and mouths

at Wednesday's
evening meal
is already in the shop,
one machinist per table,

even as our mother loves our hair,
even as our daughter
eyes our every word.

4. *Rivers: After the Rorschach, Before Dinner*

The night scythes down river.
At the bend of high hardwoods
day makes slow cutting. The slow
river takes the night as though
it were a pirogue easing downstream,
maybe with a sad man
poling to his house on stilts
around the bend. Could we know

the house on stilts around the bend
we would know the man has nothing
waiting for him but goods
in rooms papered in newsprint.
That is how evening comes,

though not always.
In point of fact, somewhere
there is a man.
At the exact moment of the metaphor,
he stops, watches where night
holds off at the bend,
where night lets the tops of the hardwoods
stay gold a little longer. He rests
or prays. He stays like this
until the bend goes dark,
darker than the rest of the river,
being the last light
not of his own making tonight.
He poles toward that dark,
knowing the river well
and the bend to his house.

This is not, of course, the first
river but another river.
It covers two states.
It changes names
two miles from his place.

5. *Open Curtain*

After three days
you open the curtain.
Behind you
a night of it
in the commons.
Three play ping-pong,
one cries in the wall.

You stretch to the gathers,
bat to make a space
your shoulders can fit.
There was an easier way,
but the cord has been removed
for those before you
or after you
who would use it
against themselves.

Through your reflected face
across the dark space
you know to be the marsh,
there is the well-lit interchange
off the by-pass. People take it
to get home from their day
shifts at the shipyard
or to leave home behind
to make it to their night
shifts. The window is hazy,

but they do not seem
to take their exits fast
or slow. From here,
being at some distance,
they seem to travel
a steady speed,
all equal. But despite *seems*,
framed in the curtain,
you know enough of the outside
to know that not all
are accounted for by one
dumb exit, not all
are going home
or leaving home.

6. *Rain*

All day it stops
and stops. No end
in sight. Glenn
is getting worse.
Allyson lets her lunch
time go, sleeping
standing up, thermostat
for a pillow.

We are not all
in such shape. But
there is something wrong
in the interminable
clear spots

of time and space,
rain on the children's unit
but clear on our smoke break benches.
Then vice versa.

One thing,
though, we can agree on
in the commons: It
comes down. It
really comes down.
After two days
of it, the inevitable:

Glenn goes to his room.

He will lose his blue card
over this. He will drop
to a red card
until we get, say,
three clear days
in a row.

7. *Bedtime*

Through the half-light of lights out,
the willing are called to an interior room,
leave Clue unsolved, its make-do
weapons—the blue chewed thing
from a Bic pen, paper clip:
It was _____, in the _____, with a Tums.

Those game for a night of sleep
will try anything. After all,
we tried anything on the outside,
swilling the tapes of *Victory At Sea*
or toward the end, napping at dawn,
Westend, in efficiencies
crawling with first names.

So we gather like partisans
at the door of the dark sound room
with our pass word, *yes*.
(*Are you up on your medicines?*
Does Mary have your vitals for the night?)

Walter, our host voice this evening,
waits, cowled in the green glow
of the stereo. In the odd dark,
we design ourselves on the wall
then the wall-to-wall mat, lying flat,
allowing ourselves space between our
selves to let tonight's recording
do its work, usually a kind of water.

Tonight the sea. Walter talks us through
its washing among the grottos we are,
folding itself in our tightening,
our letting go, and always the smooth
exhale. Then lets us go back to our rooms

where despite what is best for us,
despite the session and all the night's voice
tried to do with the sea, we may, if we choose,
close our doors, turn on our one lamp,
and make bleating heads eating our walls—
all the shadow animals our hands can manage—
while we wait for a sleep of our own.

judy

If it comes down to choosing sides,
choose Judy. She dies like nobody
else. Besides, her father
owns the theater.
Saturday before the matinee he makes deals,
bags coins in his little office
over the arc light projection room with its empty eyes.
He sits up there owning, a bald thought
in the brain of the building, rolling change.
Let the line outside get long. This place,
Palace, is ours: lobby, mezzanine,
WOMEN, MEN—partners, with Judy there we have it all.
She's everything ever wanted in an outlaw
—quick draw, wears her sidearm cross-ways, low
and loose, tied at the knee with real leather—not
some older brother's sneaker lace.

She knows this place.
If she weren't so good at dying she might even win.
But she is so good at dying.
Gut shot, she digs her fist in her stomach,
twists her own breath loose,

pulls herself up by the marble table with the dried
arrangement, drags her leg down the hall,
falls back against the gold mirror.
You move in to take her, dead or alive.
In the stand-off, behind her in the glass
you see your hat brim around her face
as though you were behind her,
facing yourself beyond her lolling tongue:
(You have had terrible dreams like this, only you were the one at
    the end of the hall, and who or what that was with hat
    brought your mother to you with water and light.)

She grips the gold frame, swings
herself against the wall like a door opening,
and now you see exactly how you look
ready to plug yourself.
She rolls into the balcony, then . . . then
over! Over the balcony! Game over?
No. Below she's taking your shots again,
coughing row by row. She takes you with her
as she goes down against the sandy white arroyo of the screen.

Is that dying, or what?

Her old man's bumping around
behind the eyes, loading the reels. This is the last killing
before the doors open
—the final death of the day except the ones we live
through on the screen. They are free.
Si, mis compadres. See gringos?
If Judy doesn't play, nobody plays.

letting the rabbit scream

You have to know what you're looking for.
It's not always those bright red eyes shining.
Sometimes a rabbit's just a piece of land
moving on the edges of your lights
on that old pile of junk you call a jeep.

But you've brought more rabbit home than I have words
to tell you how. You might be missing something,
though. Other things out there. Fiercer.

No matter what your mother says, it's time
you took that angel off your wall and the thing
with all the *If*s about being a man.
Put something up you haven't memorized—
fox, lynx. There could still be wolf.

Up to now whenever you've wounded rabbit,
shot almost where he was and hit his hip,
you've gripped his back legs and slammed his head
on the winch welded to your bumper, right?
Most times that would be right. The suffering.
But one time let him live a little while,

since anyway most natural deaths are slow.
Cut your lights. Turn your engine off.
That thing will scream and scream and scream. Scream.

Near make you think you'll never hear again
he screams so loud. High. Long. Be still.
Let him call out to the open something good—
that lynx. We've got cats big as your brother
out there, somewhere out there. Waiting.
Listen to the screams. Wait 20 minutes.
Don't worry about the dark; your eyes will come
to see. Maybe not everything, but enough.
No matter how long 20 minutes is
you sit there, quiet. Might as well enjoy the night.
Stare, not at the stars—they'll make you blind
for when you look back down to earth—stare
at the darkest thing far off that you can find.

Then hit your lights. Find the rabbit (He
might have crawled a little ways away.)
You check by him, and then you quick look off
behind the lights for yellow eyes of things
I've said I know are somewhere on this place—
I've seen sign, I've felt them watching me—
the things worth making over. Stuffed life-like,
bristling. Teeth and claws over your bed.
You can even mount the rabbit at his feet.

You do what I say. But you know what?
There's better chance there won't be nothing there.
There might. But don't bet your savings on it.

All that waiting and listening, might be nothing more
than a cold and stove-up rabbit bled to death.
So what? So what? The lynx still lives tonight.
That doesn't mean the night itself's a waste.
Hell, you might go your whole life shooting wrong,
letting the rabbit scream, and nothing there.

his breakfast

Clear the table.
Clear the room of the table.
Clear the house of the room and the land of the house, and still
the old man would be sitting in the desert that remained
telling dust and ash, as now he tells the portions on his plate.

His memory of music and fire. All grades met
at the old Academy. The primary boys
his age had left him on the second landing.
He saw in the music room, through the smoke, the music
teachers, older girl at the upright with Miss...
before he was snatched into the older boys,
descending quickstep in their blue-ribbon silence
and perfect lines. (He never got past the grade
that saved him.) The women played
for an orderly escape, the "clean egress" of drill.
The heat. The children of the world on the far wall
browned around Jesus, and in that vaulted oven, flags moved,
pictures danced—John Philip Sousa crashed in the corner,
David and Joseph and Moses and Schubert and Puck
writhed over the slate staff full of whole notes.
Miss... she turned the pages for the beautiful

Lois-who-had-played-for-Taft-in-'12, and she
covered their heads with sheets of slow songs.
The smoking paint, drizzle of blue flame,
rained down to the cloud at their feet,
dripped onto their hands, onto the keys they played.

Mother, what were their names?—
the women who played with blistering hands,
the women who played for the children to march,
who played as they cried through their tunes?—
Mother, what were their names?
They taught music in that old house for years . . . .

No No No No! The old Academy. The fire.

lapses

God has called me to live and work
three states removed from David Petty. (Praise Him.)

Ninth and 10th grades, band practice, some practiced
while our director locked himself in the supply room
to belt down his morning supply.
Behind the timpani, Petty played me with the mallets,
would chant, *c'mon c'mon, man, c'mon, c'mon chicken shit,*
whatsa matter, hit me, hit me, whatsa matter. . . .
But I didn't know what was the matter.
I couldn't *c'mon c'mon.* Even unsaved
I turned the other cheek.
Social Studies, I would dream through my conquistadors
of painting him blue, skewering him
on a lodge pole and offering him to the god of maize.

Extra credit: If an automobile weighing 2,000 pounds travels 60 miles
per hour on a straight road, assuming no friction, how high will it
bounce when it runs over David Petty's mother?

Made friends with the enemy. Slept over.
When his breathing became heavy,
lying beside him I'd hit him at the country club,

stick a fork in his throat,
throw him on the cart of *petits fours*,
roll him out to the pool, bite off his lower lip,
tear a huge chunk of cheek out with my back teeth
while the membership looked on.
Part of the fantasy always went: The nurses
and orderlies were kind to me.

At home, (even late nights in my underwear)
I practiced for hours with my father's pistol
strapped to my hip, fast draw in the mirror at myself.

I've let all that go, of course.
Even a little chicken. . . .
I can't help it, though:
Sometimes, now, even now,
surviving the siege of the world,
I kneel at the altar, my grown daughters
on either side, accept the host in my cupped hands,
and think of one more way to kill that son-of-a-bitch.

the man with the hardest belly

I

THE MAN WITH THE HARDEST BELLY knows God
compensates his loss of limbs—legs
to knee, nub arms—with a gift
to titillate the congregations when he is delivered
from Ocala in his motor home to call us to Christ.
This handsome chunk of what was left
after he'd been shucked, he says, at 14
found God by serving himself on our tables
if we had canned corn at all in 19 and 55.

We are not members here. As Dad said, we
have our own faith. But someone spirit-filled
made Mother promise. So we're here cross-legged
on the cool ground at the river,
and my father is chosen. The Youth Director
is chosen. The man high up in Amway
is chosen. The three of them hang

THE MAN WITH THE HARDEST BELLY over the first
   branch
of the maple like a sandbag on the levee.
He pops his torso, flips, chins
to the next branch, flips, grabs a limb
with his thighs. Left nub for leverage,
he hooks another V with the back
of his head, walks on stumps up the trunk
to the next limb, flips to his belly, bends,
flips, holds with his teeth. He maneuvers
like something stained and mating
toward the top of our slide in godless biology,
or like the little dots we see inside our own eyes
on days we're morose. The thing
we've come to watch we can't watch
directly as he works toward the sun. The higher
he goes, the more we must look down to save
our eyes. We pull grass, look up and squint
to check his progress, kill an ant climbing our shoe.
Some stand to change the angle,
to keep him closer to the shaded cars.
Settling high, balanced and swaying, he preaches
from the texts painted on his motor home
under the faded "DOUBT AND DELIVERY."

        II

. . . so look with me now at Genesis, whole people, Genesis 15:1–6.
Abram. Abram was a cripple in bed, had no standing among men.
Listen to me, had no standing among men, praise God, and Moses, who

said no, not me, not me, God gave Moses what he needed. And Joshua at
their first real trial? Joshua didn't think he could do nothing. Joshua
7:1–10. I thank God my arms and legs went to your soft tummies in
'55. I was born again in that shucking machine, look at my belly, my
hard and strong belly, you could park a truck on my belly praise God,
God gives you what you need. I need a strong belly and a lithe neck to
climb trees and show you the Holy Spirit at work, and show you the
compensations of our precious Lord. Praise you, Lord. The Holy Spirit
turns my pages for me. Look at Joshua splashing dirt up in his face. I'm
here to tell you people there's no dirt in my face, no Lord. And Gideon.
It's right there in your book. Judges 6:1–14. What does God say to that
worthless garment of feces? (Excuse me, ladies, but the compensations of
God is nothing to be delicate about.) Says to Gideon, go in your power.
Go in your power. Listen to me now: Go in your power and save my
people. Read it. Isn't that what it says? Your power. Don't look at me, I
know I'm pretty. Look at your book, look at your own Holy Word. Now
examine, if you will, First Corinthians 10:13. See? God won't give
you nothing wrong without a correlational power to get out of it . . . .
Jesus himself, his wonderment self, take this cup from my lips, listen
now, take this cup from my lips, take this cup . . . .

III

We pull off the road to let the other cars by.
The Youth Director finds a wide place.
And the man high up in Amway finds a wide place.
The three of us wait, our hazard lights blinking,
while the born again wave and the kids shout
from their windows that Jesus is the One
and fathers honk (Honk If You Love Jesus).

My father nods occasionally. My sister starts
it. We are arguing about whether
THE MAN WITH THE HARDEST BELLY crawls on all
four nubs around the rooms of his scriptural
motor home, or slithers like something run over.
Crawls. Slithers. My father hushes us. My sister hits
me, says, "For unto you is born *a child*." I hit
my sister: "Let the women keep silent
in the Chevrolet." My mother has had enough.
She separates us. We aren't to speak. We aren't
to utter a peep. Each of us must look out our own window.

IV

The cars are thinning. We can hear the hazards now.
The road is dark and the dust is settling.
"I told her we'd go, and we went," my mother says.
"I told you we'd come, and we came," my father says.
"I thought it a bit much, though," she says, "when
he stood on his perch, spread those arms
and screamed, 'Nail me. Nail me.'"
"Me too," my father says, "nails wouldn't work."
My mother is looking at him. He says,
"Toggle bolts might work."
"Go help him down," my mother says, "and let's go home."

My father joins the other two on the road. They walk
back toward the river. My mother tells us it will
turn cool; we don't need to bathe when we get home,

but we do need to wash our feet. My father appears.
He eases us between the Youth Director and the man
high up in Amway. When we're on the main road
and the others have turned off, my mother says,
"I thought we'd have your mother over tomorrow.
Remind me to get a ham out when we get home."
"And corn?" my father says. "Whatever," she says.

       V

Tonight down the cold upstairs hall we hear
them laughing, my mother and father.
Tonight we hear them making love again.

the day spike eisland went home

Perhaps he remembered a joke.
It was past noon, perhaps a simple grumbling
in his belly turned him left, to home,
the funeral following the hearse in his grip
despite the law that kept waving them straight at the light.

Whatever he was thinking it wasn't Death.
He'd taken death home too often before,
all over him—in his clothes and hair and eyes—
and cursed the things he was burying with himself:
ashtrays, lamps, Phillips head for slotted screws,
and never enough paint to finish a job.
(And never enough whisky to finish the job.)
And plates left out. And night. And day.

And now he finds himself stopped
before his own house, the tiny cracker box,
dead end of Laurel. The line behind him,
each car stopped for the shoulders and hats up ahead.
From soul's side, looking down, all this
must seem like a glimmering river

winding on itself through subleased land.
Spike gets out and looks across the hood
at his wife staring from the porch, a towel
in her hands. What does he say? What
could any of us say when we've led mourners
to the blue home we hated so long
we simply gave up hating at all. *He* say?
Indeed, what of her? Saturday, off from work,
her husband out there with the hearse in the heat,
the dust cloud wafting over the both of them?
She steps back into the shadow of the doorway.
She smiles and shows him her leg. Gives
the procession the finger. Wriggles her hips.
She is so beautiful nowadays when he feels dumb.

So he will bury this guy, and he will come home.
He'll bury this guy, go by the funeral parlor,
swap vehicles, sign out until Monday, and come home.
He nods to the limousined family, gives them
the half-smile they paid for, the assurances in his eyes.
He traces the caravan on foot, block by block, back
to the end car, such distant kin the headlights are off
and the kids suck the sweet cream from cakes.
Returns, Spike does, nodding, sweeping
his hand in broad strokes, as though he were painting
the earth in bold colors. Car by car the cars
turn around, begin to snake out toward the grave—
with that rather trashy-looking, un-sad, last car first.

note for in the morning

To answer your question about what
I do when I can't join you in bed
until four or so: Sometimes I read
maps. I trace a highway, always off
from here, up, then out

a county road, stop at the tables
with the X-legs, have a beer with Chad
whose brother sent him packing from their
mother in Boca Raton. The grains
of cement stick to

his forearm as he takes a last swig
and a line of them in the blond down
of his front when he leans back to burp.
I teach in a county seat some nights.
The desks are nailed down.

But I'm not teaching. While the children
read, I am looking through the rippled
windows at dogs by the swings. No one
can find me living where I've stopped.

I've assumed a name.
They were desperate, and they had a room
in the widow's house. In deserts my leg
flares up. I pull over to nurse it.
I finish Proust in Cedar Rapids.
Please know, I don't leave

you. Bathing in the Letohatchee,
I make plans to send for you, dry off
with my shirt and see what matters now.
I end with the vein that brings me home.
I've packed the lunches

for the girls. Don't let me sleep in. Maps.
Tonight, for example, with wine, while
I waited for the rug to dry, I
read Arkansas—at least to the gray
road, east to Bird Eye.

come home

Your call to check on the kids was pure
pornography—thank you. Thank you
in your smoking, wet Seattle,
for calling me, for dropping publicly
your change down into our number
like a lost teen. Good thing.
Here among the settled states,
my mind aghast at the sheer variety
of my body, I was protruding forthright
through the glow of the Giants.
We couldn't be farther apart
unless we were together
mad as hell and logical.
Here thank God it's only miles. But many.
It was a good call
in your hurry through the chrome
and glass of the next thing on your list—
the fortnight had begun to rust.
I missed your war-dead stretch
this dawn across my side
of the bed when I returned
from pissing fairly accurately.

What was the news last night
without your ignoring it?
Not news—trivia with a hairpiece.
I've had it with the local Live-5
at 6:00. Their action reports need your banging;
their anecdotes miss your stories about everything else.
It is terrible to be able to concentrate.
It's been pitiable.
So when you called, fourth and three,
the kids upstairs asleep—
of course I was not myself,
smelling you over the wires,
the phone growing hard in my hand.

pickup

"I love my truck . . . ." —Glen Campbell

Sometimes there has been enough writing.

A tall one between my legs, plenty of smokes,
squelch off, hammer down, we're on the I
again in Alabama. This is country country
on WBAM coming to you live, neighbor.

The boy I found in Montgomery
hitchhiking with my old thumb
strikes a match to show me
L.I.F.E.
tattooed on each knuckle of his left fist
with a Bic pen in the state pen.
Another match, miles down, lights
his right wrist: *Can you read*
it? Read what this one says.
I'm driving. I can't read it.
Thirteen and a half, 13 $^{1}/_{2}$ is what. I unlock
my beer from my legs and suck the last foam.
Know what it means? You got this red truck,
and I can tell you got a real family
so you don't know what it means.

I tell him he's right. I don't know.
Twelve man jury, one judge,
and a half-ass chance. Twelve, one, a half.

Keith tells me for ten bucks he'll fight
me, for twenty I can love him
up some, for fifty, he'll go down
on me, *but my private life*
about my brother and my uncle
and my old man being charged
with kidnapping me is nobody
else's business, so don't ask.
Just don't by-God ask. I won't talk personal.
We shake hands on it.

He looks at me to the next yard stick,
mile marker 109.
He shifts his feet in the maps,
coffee cups, beer cans.
I was in for a year and nine months.
They picked me up in Alabama,
but I did my time in Florida.
Gainesville?

Gainesville, what?
The night begins to change. The hour
before light. Back home
my girls—wife, two daughters, a fixed cat—
are locked in with the alarm armed.
They would not dream I have found this Keith.

Up ahead a flatbed hauls a house.

I don't know about no Gainesville.
I just know I was somewhere in Florida.
But see, it was dark when the state delivered me
and it was dark when they took me home.
So I don't know. Might be like you say. Might
have been Gainesville. I'm always getting
screwed over by The Man,
so it might have been someplace else.
I like you, but you don't know everything.
It might have been someplace you don't know.

He takes the off-ramp at Ft. Deposit
where a man owes him money.
Hey. If you write about me and tonight
and me riding with you in your red truck,
I hope you make a million dollars.

The house passes us.
I pop another beer and head on south,
find my station again.
Damn fine truck—
my Beatrice. My Linda Ronstadt.
My whining wide red woman.

tattoo #47,
"happy dragon"

Through the crawl space
of the home that will have to do us,
at least until the kids go off,
trying to tighten the jacks
to shore up our giving floor,

I've pulled the light with the long cord
fed from inside loose. I didn't know
I had been staring at the blue dragon.
After nearly 30 years it sleeps deep
and dull under the scaly skin of my arm.
I hadn't thought I was looking at anything,
but in the surprising dark, the face lit,
lifted off my arm and went with my eyes
to the corners. Pensacola, '64, the only time
I did another guy. At Gulf's edge,

those early years, those treacherous
shallows of war—we drank too many beers
and walked away from town on his pass,
six-packs cooling our burning arms.

There was a fog, up or down the beach—
up, say—hovering head high.
It drew us in.
We laughed about something or other.
(He knew he was not coming back—
like all who went, or didn't.

Nobody ever made it back from then, I guess.)
Our too loud laughs hacked against the surf.
Foam spewed from our nostrils. We dropped
to our knees in the clear below the cloud,
saw for ourselves the long light
of water down the waves
to the lights we came from. He wept
because—I don't know why he wept.
Nor how we went from that to all the other.
Or how we sobered up enough to ever feel
our way back to familiar streets.

Light: My wife
has found the pulled plug in our bedroom.
Screw it—that, and that war, wars to come.
Screw the jacks up tighter to the frame.
Dragon's as dull as ever, dim as I'd remembered—
should have had the tacky thing removed,
except the scar. "Number 47, 'Happy Dragon'":
You never drink so much you forget a thing like that,
like your own voice ordering your own tattoo.
I'm not sure what that other fellow chose.

even the sparrow has found a home

When his wife came up from the solution
in the darkness of the safelight,
the nursing son on top of her,
all his fictions were obvious
by their absence: She was embarrassed,
the boy was simply hungry.
But he had such a picture in his head
of them when he'd posed them
and when he was sipping neat rum
in the brittle bouquet of developer,
he'd get maudlin, teary at the sight of it.
But no matter what the "how to" magazines said
about the art of lighting the body—this reflector,
this angle, this, and this lens, *f*-stop,
and this time, and this—
it all developed into fact.
His series for peace looked only like his wife
staring out a window at nothing,
trying to cry. Her sad news from the war,
seemed the receipt it was.

And the rain on the window (his garden hose)
did not moisten her sweet, performing face, shadowed it.
He would sip from a cup, stare into the pan
until the ping of the timer said, bring them up,
wash them—let's see what we've got.
But every batch was botched, blotched with real life.
It got to where he knew they'd come up cold.

It got to where he didn't want to bring them up at all.
He wanted to drift down to them.
He wanted to speak into them, lay on them
like Elisha on the boy in Second Kings—
mouth to mouth, eyes to eyes, hands to hands—
until they turned warm beneath him.

The house settled,
and the world seeped in like a light leak:
yard hat on the enlarger,
huge mitt with the ice scraper,
sprung oil wrench, a thousand yards of monofilament
off the spool, an empty spool—
junk clotting in coat hangers.
Like a bad kid from a good home,
the clutter became a thing on its own,
grown out of itself, running him out.

You don't just one day quit your chosen art.
One day you speak,
admit you quit some time back

as though it were an after-thought, a fact.
The spoken word becomes the day
you start to live again.

One night he came out of the darkroom late,
an incorrigible failure,
the house cold, closed up and dark.
He climbed the stairs to them sleeping.
He smelled their warm breath in that dark.
His eyes adjusted. The shadows gave him the room.
He started to go back down,
sleep on the couch again not to disturb them.
But no. He had quit photography months—years?—ago.
How easy they moved over for him with his lightest touch of the
    bed.
Tomorrow he would break the seals of that room
—window and door—let light run riot,
get rid of everything.
Get rid of everything except the magazines.
Those he would box in the basement.
Let the colors fade, the contrasts bleed.
Let the shadowy breasts, the sparkling abdomens
with water and rock mildew among the ads.
Then, perchance, let this angel son, later,
find a private use for them, alone, in his own dark room.